The WORD LOVER'S JOURNAL

A DO-IT-YOURSELF DICTIONARY
of YOUR FAVORITE WORDS

Avon, Massachusetts

Copyright © 2011 by F+W Media, Inc.
All rights reserved.
This book, or parts thereof, may not be reproduced in any form without permission from the publisher; exceptions are made for brief excerpts used in published reviews.

Published by
Adams Media, a division of F+W Media, Inc.
57 Littlefield Street, Avon, MA 02322. U.S.A.
www.adamsmedia.com

ISBN 10: 1-4405-2890-X
ISBN 13: 978-1-4405-2890-3

Printed in the United States of America.

10 9 8 7 6 5 4 3 2 1

This publication is designed to provide accurate and authoritative information with regard to the subject matter covered. It is sold with the understanding that the publisher is not engaged in rendering legal, accounting, or other professional advice. If legal advice or other expert assistance is required, the services of a competent professional person should be sought.

—From a *Declaration of Principles* jointly adopted by a Committee of the American Bar Association and a Committee of Publishers and Associations

Many of the designations used by manufacturers and sellers to distinguish their product are claimed as trademarks. Where those designations appear in this book and Adams Media was aware of a trademark claim, the designations have been printed with initial capital letters.

inkwell © clipart.com

*This book is available at quantity discounts for bulk purchases.
For information, please call 1-800-289-0963.*

INTRODUCTION

For word lovers, there's no greater joy than that of finding a new word to add to your personal vernacular. But how many times have you heard a new word at a soirée or read a new word while browsing online and then, as you stopped to recollect later on, found that the word had been promptly consigned to oblivion?

With *The Word Lover's Journal,* logophiles finally have a place to put all these hard-to-remember words for safekeeping. If you hear a word you love, write it down. If there's a word you want to remember to define, write it down. And if you're just looking for a place to learn new words and how to use them, then do that writing here as well.

Within the pages of this journal, you'll find questions that are posed to spark creative thinking by drawing upon the words, expressions, quotes, and ideas of the cognoscenti of literature, mythology, philosophy, and other disciplines throughout history. Each entry is designed to pique your curiosity, point out new words, and prompt you to write. After all, from the erudite pleasures of an obtuse turn of phrase to the postmodern thrill of a newly coined acronym, the search for the perfect word is a hunt worth recording.

So pick up your pen, and document your love of language—one word at a time!

*To have another language
is to possess a second soul.*

—CHARLEMAGNE, KING OF THE FRANKS AND ROMAN EMPEROR

Write three of the longest foreign-language words you know and use them in sentences.

NEW WORD OF THE DAY:
anticonstitutionnellement

A man's character may be learned from the adjectives which he habitually uses in conversation.
—MARK TWAIN, AMERICAN WRITER AND HUMORIST

Which vibrant, evocative adjectives would you use to paint a word picture for a colorful character in your family or circle of friends?

NEW WORDS OF THE DAY:
voluble and *garrulous*

> *The most dangerous word in any human tongue is the word for brother. It's inflammatory.*
> —Tennessee Williams, American writer

Make a list of words that you consider provocative and alongside them, list emotionally neutral words that could be substituted.

NEW WORDS OF THE DAY:
incendiary and *seditious*

When written in Chinese, the word "crisis" is composed of two characters. One represents danger and the other represents opportunity.
—JOHN F. KENNEDY, AMERICAN PRESIDENT

Write an exotic word in which the first and second parts possess different meanings. How do these juxtaposed meanings set the word apart?

NEW WORDS OF THE DAY:
lickspittle and *pfeffernusse*

*Quirky is sexy, like scars or chipped teeth.
I also like tattoos. They're rebellious.*
—Jennifer Aniston, American television and motion picture actress

Which words would you choose to get inked?

NEW WORDS OF THE DAY:
dougie and *indelible*

Suit the action to the word, the word to the action.
—WILLIAM SHAKESPEARE, ENGLISH DRAMATIST

Write a dramatic scene for a play, short story, novel, or screenplay using only action verbs—avoiding all conjugations of the verb "to be."

NEW WORDS OF THE DAY:
vituperate and *recrudesce*

> *Why need I volumes, if one word suffice.*
> —RALPH WALDO EMERSON,
> AMERICAN PHILOSOPHER, ESSAYIST, AND POET

 *List* ten single words that do the work of two, for example, write "ascend" for going up, "pluviometer" for rain gauge, or "homebound" for going home.

1. _____
2. _____
3. _____
4. _____
5. _____
6. _____
7. _____
8. _____
9. _____
10. _____

NEW WORD OF THE DAY:
euphuism

Metaphors are dangerous. Love begins with a metaphor . . . at the point when a woman enters her first word into our poetic memory.

—Milan Kundera, Franco-Czech novelist

"People who live in glass houses shouldn't throw stones"; "a bird in the hand is worth two in the bush"; "you can lead a horse to water but you can't make him drink"; and, "America is a melting pot" are metaphors that, when jumbled together, don't make any sense. Record your favorite metaphors and write a new one.

NEW WORD OF THE DAY:
catachresis

> *"Worry" is a word that I don't allow myself to use.*
> —Dwight D. Eisenhower, American president and five-star general

List the words you avoid using and record the reasons why.

NEW WORDS OF THE DAY:
dispiteous and *eudaemonia*

The deeper the experience of an absence of meaning—in other words, of absurdity—the more energetically meaning is sought.

—VACLAV HAVEL, CZECH PLAYWRIGHT, POET, AND POLITICIAN

Record an experience in which a speaker conversed with you using words that obscured his or her message and meaning to the point of absurdity. Describe the consequences of this confusion, if any.

NEW WORDS OF THE DAY:
obnubilate and *obscurantism*

> *Every creature is a word of God.*
> —Meister Eckhardt, German theologian, philosopher, and mystic

 *List* all the names, titles, monikers, and metaphors for God that you can recall having ever heard, read, or spoken, and write a prayer using your favorites.

Names:

Your Prayer:

NEW WORDS OF THE DAY:
homoiousian and *modiolus*

A simile, to be perfect, must both illustrate and ennoble the subject.
—SAMUEL JOHNSON, ENGLISH AUTHOR, ESSAYIST, POET, CRITIC, AND LEXICOGRAPHER

 *Write* an illustrative simile to finish the following sentences:

The thunderous clapping of the drummer's palm against the *djembe* hide compelled the dancers to gyrate and jump at a feverish pace like:

The violinist's masterful bowing rendered mellifluous music that undulated like:

NEW WORDS OF THE DAY:
bodhran, spiccato, and *zouk*

Your words are my food, your breath my wine.
—SARAH BERNHARDT, FRENCH ACTRESS

 *Think* of ten words that nourish your spirit and write them into an affirmation of your brilliance.

1.	6.
2.	7.
3.	8.
4.	9.
5.	10.

NEW WORDS OF THE DAY:
proscenium and *oenophile*

Words are the voice of the heart.
—CONFUCIUS, CHINESE THINKER AND SOCIAL PHILOSOPHER

Write a love letter with a statement that clearly expresses your heartfelt, tender feelings for another person, place, or thing.

NEW WORDS OF THE DAY:
relume, agape, and *bhakti*

> *All philosophy lies in two words, "sustain" and "abstain."*
> —Epictetus, Greek Stoic philosopher

List ten of your favorite philosophical terms and use them in a short essay that expresses your "love of wisdom" (the literal meaning of philosophy).

1. _____
2. _____
3. _____
4. _____
5. _____
6. _____
7. _____
8. _____
9. _____
10. _____

NEW WORDS OF THE DAY:
ataraxia and *dogmatism*

*There are words worse than cuss words,
there are words that hurt.*

—TILLIE OLSEN, AMERICAN NOVELIST AND WRITER

Write down words in your internal dialogue or words spoken by others that inflict pain—and replace those words with new ones that lighten your heart.

NEW WORDS OF THE DAY:
piteous, perfunctory, and *perspicuous*

The quick brown fox jumps over the lazy dog.
—AN 1885 ENGLISH-LANGUAGE PANGRAM

Write your version of the perfect pangram, defined by Webster's *New World Dictionary* as a sentence that contains all the letters of the alphabet.

NEW WORD OF THE DAY:
anagram

> *Broadly speaking, short words are the best and old words the best of all.*
> —WINSTON CHURCHILL, ENGLISH STATESMAN

 List ten short words in today's vernacular that were spoken before the first century.

1. _____
2. _____
3. _____
4. _____
5. _____
6. _____
7. _____
8. _____
9. _____
10. _____

NEW WORDS OF THE DAY:
ephod and *koine*

> *Revision is one of the exquisite
> pleasures of writing.*
>
> —BERNARD MALAMUD,
> AMERICAN NOVELIST AND SHORT STORY WRITER

Compose a paragraph about the pleasurable feelings derived from writing and then revise your paragraph cutting extraneous words and clumsy constructions, and add a new word that you have never used before.

NEW WORDS OF THE DAY:
redact and *maladroit*

mouse potato (noun):
a person who spends a great deal of time using a computer.
—Merriam Webster

Which words best describe your own technological skills and activities?

NEW WORDS OF THE DAY:
webcrawler and *cyberslacker*

Euphemisms are unpleasant truths wearing diplomatic cologne.
—Quentin Crisp, English writer and raconteur

List four colorful euphemisms for "sex."

1.
2.
3.
4.

List three for "death."

1.
2.
3.

List two for "toilet."

1.
2.

List one for "deceiver."

1.

NEW WORDS OF THE DAY:
ambassadorial and *olfactory*

A man's life of any worth is a continual allegory—and very few eyes can see the mystery of his life—a life like the scriptures, figurative . . .
—JOHN KEATS, ENGLISH ROMANTIC POET

Which key words would you use to write an allegory for your own belief about life?

NEW WORDS OF THE DAY:
aphorism and *simulacrum*

> *All slang is metaphor, and all metaphor is poetry.*
> —G. K. CHESTERTON, ENGLISH-BORN, GABONESE CRITIC, ESSAYIST, NOVELIST, AND POET

Write your favorite slang word for "excrement" and include it in a political polemic or poem.

NEW WORDS OF THE DAY:
mierda (a Spanish-language word) and *scatology*

Words in proper places, make the true definition of style.

—JONATHAN SWIFT, ANGLO-IRISH SATIRIST, ESSAYIST, AND POLITICAL PAMPHLETEER

Write a passage in your favorite literary style, putting each word in its proper place; then, mix up all the words you used and write something different.

NEW WORD OF THE DAY:
adroitness

All perception of truth is the detection of an analogy.
—Henry David Thoreau, American author, poet, and naturalist

Write a statement of truth and then compose an analogy to illustrate.

NEW WORDS OF THE DAY:
verisimilitude and *mendacity*

> *There is a great power in words*
> *if you don't hitch too many of them together.*
> —JOSH BILLINGS, AMERICAN COMEDIAN

Make a list of your favorite "power" words and use them sparingly in short sentences for greatest impact.

NEW WORDS OF THE DAY:
logorrhea and *prolixity*

> *When you talk to the half wise, twaddle; when you talk to the ignorant, brag; when you talk to the sagacious, look very humble and ask their opinion.*
> —Edward G. Bulwer-Lytton, English politician, poet, and novelist

From the English language lexicon that provides myriad options for *twaddling*, *bragging*, and *opining*, which phrases are your favorites for each purpose?

NEW WORD OF THE DAY:
taciturn

> *Better than a thousand hollow words*
> *is one word that brings peace.*
> —SIDDHARTHA GAUTAMA, THE BUDDHA

Write your favorite word for restoring harmony and tranquility in times of turmoil and write a short paragraph about why that word has power, the kind of power it wields, and how peace is achieved through the use of that word.

NEW WORDS OF THE DAY:
placate and *assuage*

> *The pen is mightier than the sword.*
> —Edward G. Bulwer-Lytton, English politician, poet, and novelist

What favorite words have you used to strike a blow mightier than the sword?

NEW WORDS OF THE DAY:
emasculate, titillate, and *eviscerate*

quotation (noun):
the act of repeating erroneously the words of another.
—AMBROSE BIERCE, AMERICAN AUTHOR AND SATIRIST;
THE DEVIL'S DICTIONARY

 *Record* a favorite funny quotation that repeats an incorrect statement.

"

"

NEW WORD OF THE DAY:
specious

> *Language
> is wine upon the lips.*
> —Virginia Woolf, English Modernist writer

 *List* ten words associated with oenology.

1. ....
2. ....
3. ....
4. ....
5. ....
6. ....
7. ....
8. ....
9. ....
10. ....

NEW WORDS OF THE DAY:
lingua franca and *colloquialism*

Summer afternoon, summer afternoon, to me those are the two most beautiful words in the English language.
—HENRY JAMES, AMERICAN EXPATRIATE WRITER

Which two English words
do you believe are worthy of such praise?

1.

2.

NEW WORDS OF THE DAY:
languorous and *halcyon*

Writing is like getting married.
One should never commit oneself until one is amazed at one's luck.
—IRIS MURDOCH, BRITISH NOVELIST AND PHILOSOPHER

Write words you associate with marriage, commitment, and luck.

Marriage	Commitment	Luck

NEW WORDS OF THE DAY:
kismet, *levirate,* and *deus ex machina*

If you talk to a man in a language he understands, that goes to his head. If you talk to him in his language, that goes to his heart.
—NELSON MANDELA, SOUTH AFRICAN PRESIDENT

Record an instance when a dry, intellectual argument did nothing to win you over but the same position restated in a different way opened a pathway into your heart.

NEW WORDS OF THE DAY:
extrapolate and *propitiate*

> *I am ready to meet my Maker.*
> *Whether my Maker is prepared for the ordeal*
> *of meeting me is another matter.*
> —WINSTON CHURCHILL, ENGLISH STATESMAN

List and discuss your funniest phrase or literary expression for death.

NEW WORDS OF THE DAY:
eponymous and *posthumous*

A Frenchwoman, when double-crossed, will kill her rival; the Italian woman would rather kill her deceitful lover; the English woman simply breaks off all relations, but they all will console themselves with another man.

—CHARLES BOYER, FRENCH ACTOR

Which words would you use to portray a deceitful lover? Why choose these particular words?

NEW WORDS OF THE DAY:
chicanery and *philanderer*

*Clutter is the disease of American writing.
We are a society strangling in unnecessary words,
circular constructions, pompous frills, and meaningless jargon.*
—William Zinsser, American writer, editor, and teacher

List ten words or expressions that, when eliminated, would improve our society's verbal and written skills.

1. ⎯
2. ⎯
3. ⎯
4. ⎯
5. ⎯
6. ⎯
7. ⎯
8. ⎯
9. ⎯
10. ⎯

NEW WORDS OF THE DAY:
obfuscators, stupefy, and *befuddle*

*The first symptom of love in a young man is shyness;
the first symptom in a woman, it's boldness.*
—Victor Hugo, French Romantic poet, novelist, and dramatist

Write your favorite pairs of antonyms and use them in sentences about falling in love.

Antonyms:

NEW WORDS OF THE DAY:
attenuate and *intensify*

> *Intellectual "work" is misnamed. It is a pleasure, dissipation, and its own highest reward.*
> —MARK TWAIN, AMERICAN WRITER AND HUMORIST

Which words pique your interest, fire your imagination, and compel you to follow some intellectual pursuit, curiosity, and anticipation of learning something new?

NEW WORDS OF THE DAY:
acculturation and *edification*

*Forgiveness is a funny thing.
It warms the heart and cools the sting.*
—WILLIAM ARTHUR WARD, AMERICAN INSPIRATIONAL WRITER

For each of the following options write a single sentence containing:

A hot, passionate apology.

A cold, calculated apology.

A rhapsodic apology.

NEW WORDS OF THE DAY:
remorseful and *contrition*

Myth is the hidden part of every story, the buried part, the region that is still unexplored because there are as yet no words to enable us to get there. Myth is nourished by silence as well as by words.
—ITALO CALVINO, ITALIAN JOURNALIST, NOVELIST, AND SHORT STORY WRITER

Use your favorite mythological hero or heroine as the protagonist of a new story.

NEW WORDS OF THE DAY:
chthonic and *ennead*

For me, a page of good prose is where one hears the rain and the noise of battle.

—JOHN CHEEVER, AMERICAN WRITER AND WINNER OF THE NATIONAL MEDAL FOR LITERATURE, 1982

Create a list of your favorite homonyms—words that sound alike, but are spelled differently.

NEW WORDS OF THE DAY:
moiré and *moray*

> *When we speak the word "life," it must be understood that we are not referring to life as we know it from its surface of fact, but to that fragile, fluctuating center which forms never reach.*
> —ANTONIN ARTAUD, FRENCH PLAYWRIGHT, POET, AND ACTOR

Which words would you use to describe the essence of life?

NEW WORDS OF THE DAY:
panspermia theory and *biopoesis*

*I have never developed indigestion
from eating my words.*
—Winston Churchill, English statesman

Write a funny story about when you or someone you know made a public statement and was proven wrong.

NEW WORDS OF THE DAY:
braggart and *ignominious*

Only the Irish have remained incomparable conversationalists, maybe because technical progress has passed them by.
—ORSON WELLES, AMERICAN ACTOR, DIRECTOR, PRODUCER, AND WRITER

List ten titillating, tantalizing, and evocative words that can be incorporated into suggestive statements guaranteed to entice others into conversation.

1.
2.
3.
4.
5.
6.
7.
8.
9.
10.

NEW WORDS OF THE DAY:
incommensurable, flagrante delicto, and *imbroglio*

> *Retirement is the ugliest word in the language.*
> —ERNEST HEMINGWAY, AMERICAN WRITER AND NOBEL LAUREATE

Write down the ten words that you hold as the ugliest in the English language.

1. _____
2. _____
3. _____
4. _____
5. _____
6. _____
7. _____
8. _____
9. _____
10. _____

NEW WORDS OF THE DAY:
grotesque and *ponderous*

> *Beauty?...*
> *To me it is a word without sense because*
> *I do not know where its meaning comes*
> *from or where it leads to.*
>
> —Pablo Picasso, Spanish artist

List several words you believe to be without sense or, in essence, bankrupt because they lack meaning without context?

NEW WORDS OF THE DAY:
inchoate and *arcane*

*Speak when you are angry,
and you'll make the best speech you'll ever regret.*
—Dr. Laurence J. Peter, American educator and writer

Which words do you most often blurt out in a fit of anger knowing that sooner or later you'll regret using them?

NEW WORDS OF THE DAY:
unctuous, disgorge, and *harangue*

*Ignorance is the curse of God;
knowledge is the wing wherewith we fly to heaven.*
—William Shakespeare, English dramatist and playwright

Which words must be included in any curse or any blessing for them to sound powerful?

Curse...	Blessing...

NEW WORDS OF THE DAY:
anathema and *denunciation*

Duty is the most sublime word in our language. Do your duty in all things. You cannot do more. You should never wish to do less.
—ROBERT E. LEE, AMERICAN CIVIL WAR GENERAL

Which duties would you just as soon abnegate? Why?

NEW WORDS OF THE DAY:
obligatory, de rigueur, and *discretionary*

> *The greatest way to live with honor in this world is to be what we pretend to be.*
> —SOCRATES, GREEK PHILOSOPHER

List six words that best describe the way you would like the world to perceive you.

1. _____
2. _____
3. _____
4. _____
5. _____
6. _____

NEW WORDS OF THE DAY:
ebullient and *inexorable*

The source of genius is imagination alone, the refinement of the senses that sees what others do not see, or sees them differently.
—Eugéne Delacroix, French Romantic artist

Compose a statement a variety of adjectives and nouns that best reflect a sense of your genius.

NEW WORDS OF THE DAY:
quintessential and *epitomize*

*Inspiration and genius—
one and the same.*

—Victor Hugo, French Romantic poet, novelist, and dramatist

Which are your favorite interchangeable words?

NEW WORDS OF THE DAY:
iniquitous and *nefarious*

> *If you do not tell the truth about yourself*
> *you cannot tell it about other people.*
>
> —VIRGINIA WOOLF, ENGLISH MODERNIST WRITER

Which evocative words would you use to write a scene from your life story that is emotionally rather than factually accurate?

NEW WORDS OF THE DAY:
memoirist and *memesis*

> *All our words are but crumbs that fall from the feast of the mind.*
> —KAHLIL GIBRAN, LEBANESE-BORN AMERICAN ARTIST, POET, AND WRITER

Create your own food-related metaphor using the quote above as inspiration.

NEW WORDS OF THE DAY:
inappetence and *satiated*

> *Nothing's beautiful from every point of view.*
> —Horace, Roman poet

Write about your best attribute and worst flaw from the first-person point of view.

NEW WORDS OF THE DAY:
perspicacious and *Janus*

He who has a why to live can bear almost any how.
—Friedrich Nietzsche, German philosopher

What words would you use to describe the whys and hows of your life's greatest challenges?

NEW WORDS OF THE DAY:
alacrity and *morose*

Even a happy life cannot be without a measure of darkness, and the word "happy" would lose its meaning if it were not balanced by sadness. It is far better to take things as they come along with patience and equanimity.
—CARL GUSTAV JUNG, SWISS PSYCHIATRIST
AND FOUNDER OF ANALYTICAL PSYCHOLOGY

Write down the words that symbolize the darkest dark of human experience and then record the words that serve as the counterbalance of light.

NEW WORDS OF THE DAY:
gossamer, diaphanous, and *heureux*

> *Character is much easier kept than recovered.*
> —Thomas Paine, American author, pamphleteer, and patriot

Write your favorite satirical, pithy, and poetic statement.

NEW WORD OF THE DAY:
epigrammatism

*Two things inspire me to awe—
the starry heavens above and the moral universe within.*

—ALBERT EINSTEIN, GERMAN-BORN THEORETICAL PHYSICIST

List two words that you believe
link astronomy and humanity.

1.

2.

NEW WORDS OF THE DAY:
cosmological, casuist, and *quark*

*There was a short lady from Nepal
Who bought her pajamas, size tall.*
—ANONYMOUS

Finish the limerick above.

NEW WORDS OF THE DAY:
salwar and *kameez*

*Doubt is a pain too lonely to know
that faith is his twin brother.*

—KAHLIL GIBRAN, LEBANESE-BORN AMERICAN ARTIST, POET, AND WRITER

Which words with opposing meanings would you use to make a philosophical statement?

NEW WORDS OF THE DAY:
platitude and *postulate*

> *I want to know God's thoughts;*
> *the rest are details.*
>
> —ALBERT EINSTEIN, GERMAN-BORN THEORETICAL PHYSICIST

Consider your life goals and jot down the words that best express the big picture as well as specific details that you—the visionary creator of your life—wish for your future.

NEW WORDS OF THE DAY:
amorphous and *ostentatious*

*A world of facts lies outside and
beyond the world of words.*
—THOMAS HUXLEY, ENGLISH BIOLOGIST

Write about an experience that defies scientific explanation, but for which you have direct knowledge and hold as factually true.

NEW WORDS OF THE DAY:
hypnagogic and *solipsism*

The finest language is made up of simple unimposing words.
—George Eliot, English novelist

List your favorite nine-letter words and find shorter, simpler, and unimposing words with which to replace them.

List your favorite seven-letter words and find shorter words to replace these.

List your favorite five-letter words and choose a short synonym for each.

List your favorite three-letter words and write about whether or not you use these words more often than your favorite nine-letter words, and why or why not.

NEW WORDS OF THE DAY:
patois and *vernacular*

Amor fati, "Love your fate," which is in fact your life.
—FRIEDRICH NIETZSCHE, GERMAN PHILOSOPHER

Write as many foreign-language phrases as you can think of that are about love, fate, and acceptance.

NEW WORDS OF THE DAY:
fidelity, predetermination, and *negate*

> Yet each man kills the thing he loves, / By each let this be heard, / Some do it with a bitter look, / Some with a flattering word.
>
> —OSCAR WILDE, IRISH WRITER AND POET;
> THE BALLAD OF READING GAOL

Which words do you use to flatter and which to criticize?

Flatter	Criticize

NEW WORD OF THE DAY:
scarify

> *Wit has truth in it;*
> *wisecracking is simply calisthenics with words.*
> —Dorothy Parker, American poet and satirist

Write a witty sentence using alliteration with words starting with the letter "w."

NEW WORDS OF THE DAY:
erudite and *malapropism*

Why and how are words so important that they cannot be too often used.
—NAPOLEON BONAPARTE, FRENCH EMPEROR AND MILITARY LEADER

Which two words do you believe are important enough to be used frequently? Why do you feel that these words should be brought into everyday conversation?

NEW WORDS OF THE DAY:
marginalize and *obviate*

Words will build no walls.
—PLUTARCH, GREEK HISTORIAN AND BIOGRAPHER

Describe the tumbling of emotional barriers when you have shifted the paradigm between yourself and another person through judicious communication.

NEW WORD OF THE DAY:
unequivocal

> *Words can sometimes, in moments of grace, attain the quality of deeds.*
> —ELIE WIESEL, ROMANIAN-BORN, JEWISH-AMERICAN WRITER, PROFESSOR, ACTIVIST, AND NOBEL LAUREATE

Record your most memorable story about someone offering a word of warning, advice, forgiveness, or love and the consequence of these actions, if any.

NEW WORDS OF THE DAY:
meritorious and *eminence*

Each cough tickles my vulva.
—ANONYMOUS

Recall an occasion when you used the wrong word for a body part while discussing a medical condition and use that experience as a point of departure for writing about it.

NEW WORDS OF THE DAY:
uvula and *trachea*

Every poet knows the pun is Pierian, that it springs from the same soil as the Musea matching and shifting of vowels and consonants, an adroit assonance sometimes derided as jackassonance.
—LOUIS UNTERMEYER, AMERICAN POET AND CRITIC; *BYGONES*

Write a play on words to create a pun with a double entendre.

NEW WORDS OF THE DAY:
mnemonic and *pneumonic*

A great many people think that polysyllables are a sign of intelligence.

—BARBARA WALTERS, AMERICAN BROADCAST JOURNALIST AND AUTHOR

List ten polysyllabic words that begin with "p," as in pomposity.

1.
2.
3.
4.
5.
6.
7.
8.
9.
10.

NEW WORDS OF THE DAY:
grandiloquent and *acumen*

> *As advertising blather becomes the nation's normal idiom, language becomes printed noise.*
> —GEORGE WILL, AMERICAN COLUMNIST, JOURNALIST, AND PULITZER PRIZE WINNER

Write your favorite stylistic expression coined from *advertising blather*. Why is it your favorite?

NEW WORD OF THE DAY:
transubstantiation

Alea iacta est.
(Latin: The die has been cast.)
—Julius Caesar, Roman General and Statesman

Write your favorite foreign-language phrase that has made its way into English vernacular.

"

"

NEW WORDS OF THE DAY:
vox populi and *ex voto*

A huge dog, tied by a chain, was painted on the wall and over it was written in capital letters "Beware of the dog."
—GAIUS PETRONIUS ARBITER, ROMAN COURTIER AND PRESUMED AUTHOR OF SATYRICON

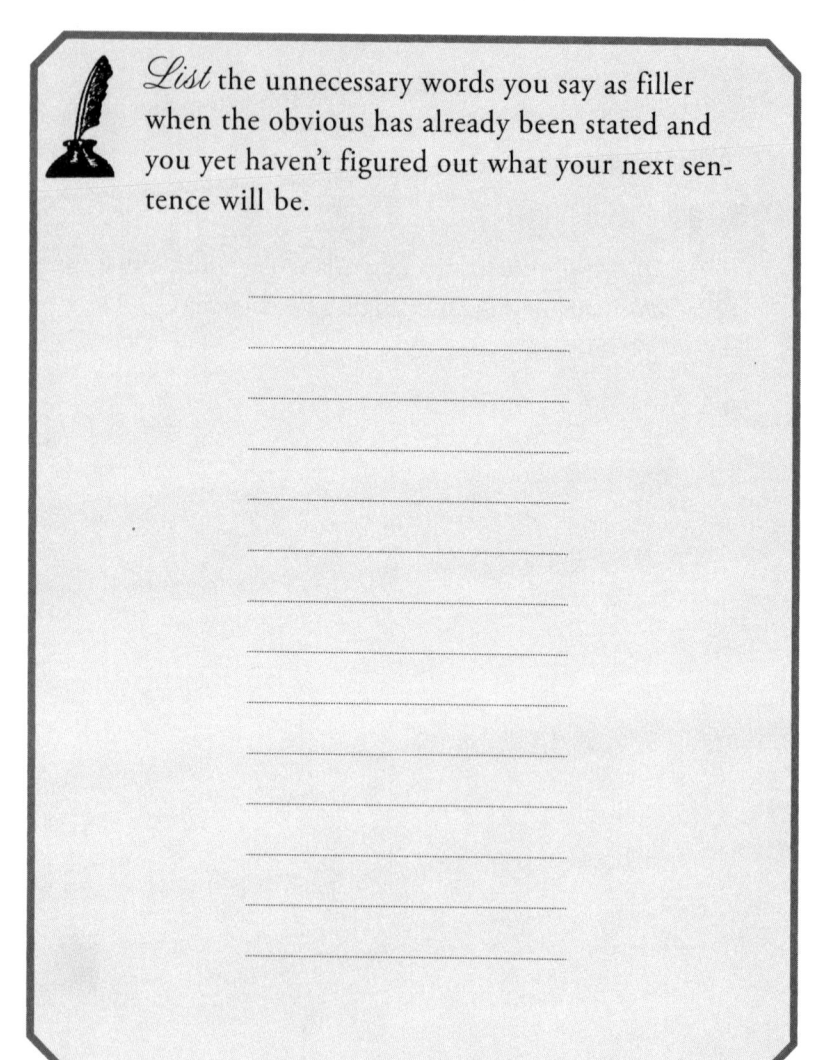

List the unnecessary words you say as filler when the obvious has already been stated and you yet haven't figured out what your next sentence will be.

NEW WORD OF THE DAY:
loquacious

> *Brevity is the soul of wit.*
> —WILLIAM SHAKESPEARE, ENGLISH DRAMATIST AND PLAYWRIGHT; *HAMLET*

Write a one-sentence epigram using as few words as possible.

....

....

....

....

....

NEW WORDS OF THE DAY:
paradoxical and *witticism*

> *It is easier to be a lover than a husband for the simple reason that it is more difficult to be witty every day than to produce the occasional bon mot.*
> —HONORE DE BALZAC, FRENCH NOVELIST

Write a clever toast for a party to announce an engagement or new love.

NEW WORD OF THE DAY:
scintillating

One great use of words is to hide our thoughts.
—VOLTAIRE, FRENCH PHILOSOPHER AND WRITER

What secret words do you ponder during private, personal moments of reflecting, remembering, or dreaming?

NEW WORD OF THE DAY:
surreptitious

The only words that ever satisfied me as describing Nature are the terms used in fairy books, charm, spell, enchantment. They express the arbitrariness of the fact and its mystery.

—G. K. Chesterton, English-born, Gabonese critic, essayist, novelist, and poet

List three words that you would use when writing about Nature, then give the reasons why you would use these words.

1.
2.
3.

NEW WORDS OF THE DAY:
riparian, palustrine, and *involucres*

I was in a queer mood, thinking myself very old: but now I am a woman again—as I always am when I write.

—Virginia Woolf, English Modernist writer

When you write, which words do you use that suggest your gender?

NEW WORDS OF THE DAY:
effeminate and *virility*

> *In three words I can sum up everything I've learned about life: it goes on.*
> —Robert Frost, American poet

Write a three-word sentence about everything you've learned about life.

_____ _____ _____

NEW WORDS OF THE DAY:
terse and *succinct*

Words are loaded pistols.
—Jean-Paul Sartre, French existentialist philosopher

List a variety of words that have the explosive power of a firearm and use them in sentences.

NEW WORDS OF THE DAY:
blunderbuss, howitzer, and *culverin*

The word "good" has many meanings. For example, if a man were to shoot his grandmother at a range of five hundred yards, I should call him a good shot, but not necessarily a good man.

—G. K. CHESTERTON, ENGLISH-BORN, GABONESE CRITIC, ESSAYIST, NOVELIST, AND POET

List the words, including prefixes and suffixes that, when added to *good*, express negative and positive meanings.

NEW WORDS OF THE DAY:
convivial and *companionable*

> *The difficulty of literature is not to write,
> but to write what you mean.*
>
> —Robert Louis Stevenson, Scottish novelist,
> poet, essayist, and travel writer

Use three new words in a well-crafted sentence that precisely expresses your feeling toward a work of classical literature.

NEW WORDS OF THE DAY:
complicatedness and *connotation*

> *The intellect has little to do on the road to discovery. There comes a leap in consciousness, call it intuition or what you will, the solution comes to you and you don't know how or why.*
> —Albert Einstein, German-born theoretical physicist

Write about your experience of an epiphany in which you discover a missing piece to a puzzle, a solution to a problem, or a sudden understanding of meaning for which you don't know the how or why.

NEW WORDS OF THE DAY:
synchronicity and *causality*

> *For some moments in life there are no words.*
> —DAVID SELTZER, AMERICAN SCREENWRITER, PRODUCER, AND DIRECTOR

Write about a time in your life when something happened that left you momentarily without words.

NEW WORDS OF THE DAY:
inarticulate and *incoherent*

Poetry is when an emotion has found its thought and the thought has found words.

—ROBERT FROST, AMERICAN POET

Write about a time when you felt a strong emotion or feeling that triggered increased attention or thought. What followed after you started to pay more attention and think more deeply about the situation?

NEW WORDS OF THE DAY:
effervescent and *repugnant*

Humor is the first of the gifts to perish in a foreign tongue.
—Virginia Woolf, English Modernist writer

Write down several foreign words whose meanings have no direct English translation. What, if anything, are we missing by not being able to translate these words?

NEW WORDS OF THE DAY:
katahara itai, Zeitgeist, and *uber*

> *Knowledge of histories / Knowledge of poetics / Knowledge of ancient verse*
>
> —WELSH TRIAD OF THINGS THAT ENLARGE THE POETIC GIFT

Write down three words taken from Celtic history.

....

....

....

Write down two words borrowed from Celtic poetry.

....

....

Compose a verse using those five words and others. Does your verse give you knowledge or a connection to those who came before?

....

....

....

NEW WORDS OF THE DAY:
incantatory and *elegies*

Lying is done with words and also with silence.
—ADRIENNE RICH, AMERICAN POET, ESSAYIST, AND FEMINIST

Write a paragraph about a time when you lied. What words did you use to circumnavigate the truth? Why did you use these particular words?

NEW WORDS OF THE DAY:
subterfuge and *beguilement*

ubicomp (noun):
*an acronym for ubiquitous computing,
that describes the various ways humans interact with
their computers, using devices such as pads, boards, and tabs.*
—Merriam Webster

Which words best describe your ubicomp activities.

NEW WORDS OF THE DAY:
MEMS and *dashboard*

The art of medicine cannot be inherited, nor can it be copied from books.

—Paracelsus, physician and alchemist

Which words would you ascribe to healing? What meaning do these words have for you?

NEW WORDS OF THE DAY:
smelting, panacea, and *elixir*

> *My name is only an anagram of toilets.*
> —T. S. ELIOT, AMERICAN-BORN ENGLISH POET, PLAYWRIGHT, LITERARY CRITIC, AND NOBEL LAUREATE

Create an anagram from either a celebrity name or your own name.

NEW WORD OF THE DAY:
los baños

*Since brass, nor stone, nor earth, nor boundless sea, /
But sad mortality o'er-sways their power.*

—WILLIAM SHAKESPEARE, ENGLISH DRAMATIST
AND PLAYWRIGHT; SONNET 65

Record your favorite use of literary incrementations, the building up of parts in a sequence until the strongest part occupies the final position.

NEW WORDS OF THE DAY:
amplification and *auxesis*

edible (adjective):
good to eat, and wholesome to digest, as a worm to a toad, a toad to a snake, a snake to a pig, a pig to a man, and a man to a worm.

—Ambrose Bierce, American author and satirist;
The Devil's Dictionary

Describe the wholesome, edible morsels you last ingested.

NEW WORDS OF THE DAY:
hors d'oeuvres, zakuskă, and *tapas*

Wealth:
any income that is at least one hundred dollars more a year than the income of one's sister's husband.

—H. L. MENCKEN, AMERICAN COLUMNIST, ESSAYIST, MAGAZINE EDITOR, AND SATIRIST

List ten foreign currencies and the countries to which they belong. Which of these currencies can you imagine using in a short story and why?

1.
2.
3.
4.
5.
6.
7.
8.
9.
10.

NEW WORDS OF THE DAY:
ouguiya, moidore, and *bitcoin*

> *The adjective hasn't been built that can pull a weak or inaccurate noun out of a tight place.*
> —WILLIAM STRUNK JR. AND E. B. WHITE;
> THE ELEMENTS OF STYLE

Write down your favorite adjectives that do more than just modify. What else do these adjectives do?

NEW WORD OF THE DAY:
flaccid

English is such a deliciously complex and undisciplined language, we can bend, fuse, distort words to all our purposes. We give old words new meanings and we borrow new words from any language that intrudes into our intellectual environment.

—WILLARD GAYLIN, AMERICAN PSYCHIATRIST AND BIOETHICIST

Which basic words forming hip, new, urban compounds are your favorites?

NEW WORDS OF THE DAY:
kindergallery and *manjibberish*

Love is a special word, and I only use it once when I mean it. You say the word too much and it becomes cheap.
—RAY CHARLES, AMERICAN MUSICIAN

What are your favorite expressions of love? Write them down and discuss their meaning.

NEW WORDS OF THE DAY:
amor, liefde, and *rakkaus*

> *A large nose is the mark of a witty, courteous,*
> *affable, generous, and liberal man.*
> —CYRANO DE BERGERAC, FRENCH DRAMATIST AND DUELIST

How would you describe an avuncular man?

NEW WORDS OF THE DAY:
mensch and *haimish*

> *Republicans understand the importance of bondage between a mother and child.*
> —DAN QUAYLE, AMERICAN VICE PRESIDENT

List your three favorite expressions in which an inappropriate or unsuitable word was used instead of the word with the correct meaning.

1.

2.

3.

NEW WORD OF THE DAY:
malapropos

Strong and bitter words indicate a weak cause.
—Victor Hugo, French Romantic poet, novelist, and dramatist

What's the last bitter word you used while defending a belief during a contentious discussion?

NEW WORDS OF THE DAY:
abdicate, abate, and *capitulate*

One merit of poetry few persons will deny: it says more and in a few words than prose.

—VOLTAIRE, FRENCH PHILOSOPHER AND WRITER

Write your favorite poem and then rewrite it in prose to prove or disprove the statement above.

NEW WORDS OF THE DAY:
iambic pentameter, caesura, and *sonneteer*

*Between men and women there is no friendship.
There is passion, enmity, worship, love, but no friendship.*
—OSCAR WILDE, IRISH WRITER AND POET

Which nouns explain your relationships with the opposite sex?

NEW WORDS OF THE DAY:
misogynist and *misandrist*

> *Mythology:*
> *the body of a primitive people's beliefs, concerning its origin, early history, heroes, deities and so forth, as distinguished from the true accounts it invents later.*
> —AMBROSE BIERCE, AMERICAN WRITER, AUTHOR, AND SATIRIST; *THE DEVIL'S DICTIONARY*

Write a myth with you as the protagonist.

NEW WORDS OF THE DAY:
mythopoeia, allegory, and *euhemerism*

> *It ain't what they call you,*
> *it's what you answer to.*
>
> —W. C. FIELDS, AMERICAN COMEDIAN

Which words would you use to define yourself? Write a paragraph in the third person using those words.

NEW WORDS OF THE DAY:
autodidactic and *thaumaturgic*

*A word, once sent abroad,
flies irrevocably.*
—HORACE, ROMAN POET

Which words do you think Search for Extra-Terrestrial Intelligence (SETI) programs should broadcast to the farthest reaches of the world, destined to join the ancient echoes of the universe? Why should those particular words be broadcast?

NEW WORDS OF THE DAY:
sagacity and *immutable*

Audacity augments courage; hesitation, fear.
—PUBLILIUS SYRUS, LATIN WRITER

Record a time when audacity emboldened you or when hesitation intensified your fear about something.

NEW WORD OF THE DAY:
bodacious

> *Kind words do not cost much.*
> *They never blister the tongue or lips.*
> —BLAISE PASCAL, FRENCH MATHEMATICIAN,
> PHYSICIST, INVENTOR, AND PHILOSOPHER

Write a recipe for happiness using ten caring and courteous words.

NEW WORDS OF THE DAY:
virtuous and *resplendent*

Words are potent weapons for all causes, good or bad.
—MANLY P. HALL, CANADIAN-BORN AUTHOR AND MYSTIC

Which fighting words would you use to defend a favorite cause?

NEW WORDS OF THE DAY:
philosophize and *proselytize*

Men would live exceedingly quiet if these two words, mine and thine, were taken away.

—ANAXAGORAS, PRE-SOCRATIC GREEK PHILOSOPHER

Which two words, once removed from the vernacular, do you believe would quiet the cacophony of humankind, and why?

1.

2.

NEW WORDS OF THE DAY:
vociferous and *raucous*

Poets are shameless with their experiences: they exploit them.
—FRIEDRICH NIETZSCHE, GERMAN PHILOSOPHER; *BEYOND GOOD AND EVIL*

Which personal life experience would you dare to exploit in a poem? Write your poem and then explain why you would exploit that particular life experience.

NEW WORDS OF THE DAY:
existentialism and *philology*

> *A man is like a fraction whose numerator is what he is and whose denominator is what he thinks of himself. The larger the denominator, the smaller the fraction.*
>
> —LEO TOLSTOY, RUSSIAN NOVELIST

Using mathematical words, how would you describe yourself, whether in parts, portions, shapes, or equations?

NEW WORDS OF THE DAY:
ellipsoid and *matrix*

> *For just when ideas fail,*
> *a word comes in to save the situation.*
> —Johann Wolfgang von Goethe, German dramatist,
> novelist, poet, and scientist

Record your most dramatic incident when an inspired word saved the day.

NEW WORDS OF THE DAY:
fortuitous and *expedient*

It is foolish to fear what you can't avoid.
—Publilius Syrus, Latin writer

List your three greatest fears and write about the consequences of avoidance.

NEW WORDS OF THE DAY:
averse and *imprudent*

For diplomacy to be effective, words must be credible....
—GEORGE W. BUSH, AMERICAN PRESIDENT

List the tired clichés bandied about by politicians and other authority figures who erroneously think these clichés boost their credibility.

NEW WORDS OF THE DAY:
bombastic and *pontificate*

> *Always give a word or sign of salute when meeting or passing a friend, or even a stranger, if in a lonely place.*
> —Tecumseh, Native American leader of the Shawnee

Which words do you favor when greeting fellow travelers dealing with the vicissitudes of life?

NEW WORDS OF THE DAY:
salutation and *ardent*

Ah, yes, divorce... from the Latin word meaning to rip out a man's genitals through his wallet.
—ROBIN WILLIAMS, AMERICAN COMEDIAN AND ACTOR

Write down your funniest story about someone's divorce... perhaps your own.

NEW WORDS OF THE DAY:
emasculate and *irreverence*

> *Failure is a word unknown to me.*
> —Muhammad Ali Jinnah, Muslim lawyer, politician, and Pakistani leader

Write down the words that are so self-limiting that you have banished them from your vocabulary and discuss why those words in particular are so offensive to you.

NEW WORD OF THE DAY:
egregious

> *It's hard not to write satire.*
> *Honesty is praised and left to shiver.*
> —JUVENAL, LATIN AUTHOR

Use your favorite prickly, pointed words to excoriate modern culture, society, beliefs, and mores.

NEW WORDS OF THE DAY:
dactylic hexameter and *rebuke*

> *Whatever you can do or dream, begin it.*
> —JOHANN WOLFGANG VON GOETHE, GERMAN DRAMATIST, NOVELIST, POET, AND SCIENTIST

In the order of importance, list three larger-than-life dreams you hope to fulfill and write a mission statement for each.

1.

2.

3.

NEW WORDS OF THE DAY:
fervent and *carpe diem*

Thy body is all vice, and thy mind all virtue.
—SAMUEL JOHNSON, ENGLISH AUTHOR, ESSAYIST, POET, CRITIC, AND LEXICOGRAPHER

Which absolutisms do you abhor? With which do you agree? Why?

NEW WORD OF THE DAY:
unchallengeable

*Mary had a little lamb, Its fleece was white as snow, /
And everywhere that Mary went / The lamb was sure to go.*

—SARAH JOSEPHA HALE; *POEMS FOR OUR CHILDREN:
"MARY'S LITTLE LAMB"* (1830)

Make a list of clichés such as "white as snow" to avoid when writing a rhyme, then put an adult spin on those clichés.

NEW WORDS OF THE DAY:
anthropomorphic and *theriomorphic*

The two most misused words in the entire English vocabulary are love and friendship. A true friend would die for you so when you start to count them on one hand, you don't need any fingers.

—LARRY FLYNT, AMERICAN PUBLISHER

Are you guilty of the misuse of specific words, and if so, which ones?

NEW WORD OF THE DAY:
solecism

> *The awful daring of a moment's surrender /*
> *Which an age of prudence can never retract /*
> *By this, and this only, we have existed.*
>
> —T. S. Eliot, American-born English poet, playwright, literary critic, and Nobel laureate; *The Waste Land*

Write a few paragraphs about an incident when you acted on impulse, without the benefit of circumspection and forethought, and the consequences, whether good or bad.

NEW WORDS OF THE DAY:
caprice, *whimsy,* and *trepidation*

Every spoken word arouses our self-will.
—JOHANN WOLFGANG VON GOETHE, GERMAN DRAMATIST, NOVELIST, POET, AND SCIENTIST

Write five words that stimulate your thoughts about your right of self-determination—the democratic right to freely express your will and influence your own future. Write about why political self-determination is or is not important to you.

NEW WORDS OF THE DAY:
sovereignty, despotism, and *autarchy*

Life is a moderately good play, with a badly written third act.
—Truman Capote, American author and comedian

As the master playwright/creator of your life, which part of the dramatic composition are you working through—the inciting incident, rising action, climax, falling action, or denouement? Write a short narrative about each and ensure the third act, if not well written, is at least is well conceived.

NEW WORDS OF THE DAY:
turgid and *lackluster*

Miracles are not contrary to nature, but only contrary to what we know about nature.
—SAINT AUGUSTINE, AFRICAN-BORN ROMAN PHILOSOPHER AND THEOLOGIAN

Record an incident that turned everything you knew about the natural world on its head.

NEW WORDS OF THE DAY:
epistemological and *empirical*

> *Colors fade, temples crumble,*
> *empires fall, but wise words endure.*
> —EDWARD THORNDIKE, AMERICAN PSYCHOLOGIST

Which words of wisdom do you call forth for comfort and meaning in times of decline, sorrow, or scarcity?

NEW WORD OF THE DAY:
psychological connectionism

Words are things, and a small drop of ink, falling like dew upon a thought, produces that which makes thousands, perhaps millions, think.
—LORD BYRON, BRITISH POET

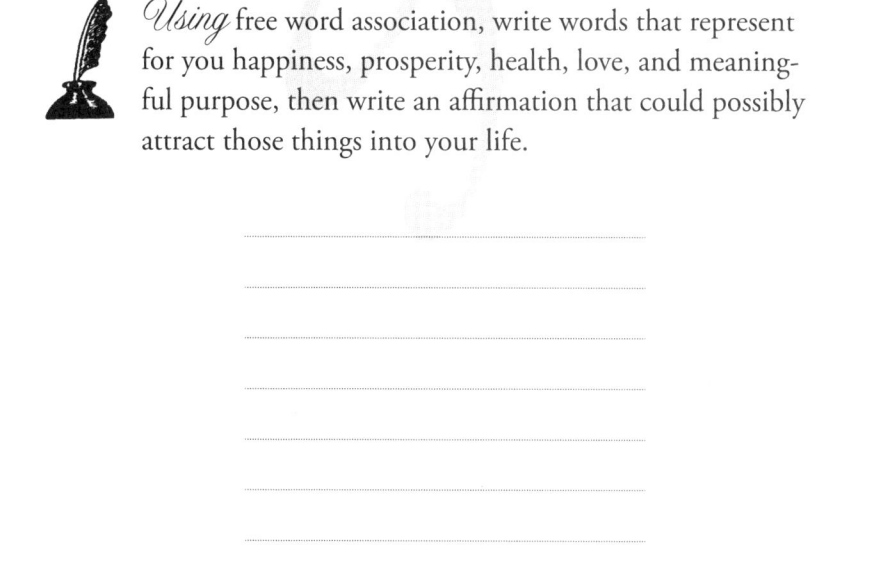

Using free word association, write words that represent for you happiness, prosperity, health, love, and meaningful purpose, then write an affirmation that could possibly attract those things into your life.

NEW WORDS OF THE DAY:
actionable and *tangible*

> *Where is the wisdom we have lost in knowledge?*
> *Where is the knowledge we have lost in information?*
>
> —T. S. Eliot, American-born English poet, playwright, literary critic, and Nobel laureate

List a variety of words in pop culture borrowed from ancient wisdom sources. Do these words retain their ancient wisdom despite their modern usage?

NEW WORDS OF THE DAY:
ambiguous and *obsolescence*

The word of man is the most durable of all material.
—Arthur Schopenhauer, German philosopher

Write a lasting epitaph for yourself or someone else.

NEW WORDS OF THE DAY:
sustantivo, necrología, and *obiturio*

> *Speak clearly, if you speak at all;*
> *carve every word before you let it fall.*
> —Oliver Wendell Holmes, American Jurist
> and Associate Justice of the U.S. Supreme Court

List five words of legalese that illustrate why few people care to read legal documents. Write a sentence using each of these words in negative fashion.

1. _____

2. _____

3. _____

4. _____

5. _____

NEW WORDS OF THE DAY:
prima facie and *sequestration*

How often have I said to you that when you have eliminated the impossible, whatever remains, however improbable, must be the truth?
—Sherlock Holmes to Dr. Watson;
The Sign of Four, Sir Arthur Conan Doyle (1890)

Write a humorous declaration or discovery of truth for your life such as, "With joy, I anticipated the golden years but getting old isn't for sissies, and the predominate color isn't gold at all but silvery gray." Or, "Forget Mars and Venus—men are from Earth and women are from Earth, unless you believe in extraterrestrials." Use your truth to write a scene for your memoir that illustrates or gives meaning to how you arrived at that truth.

NEW WORDS OF THE DAY:
nonchalance and *deductive reasoning*

Who in the world am I?
Ah, that is the great puzzle.

—Lewis Carroll (aka Charles Ludwidge Dodgson), English author, mathematician, Anglican deacon, and photographer

Which words would you use to sum up the essence of who you are? Alternatively, which words would you use to reinvent yourself, projecting a new persona for the world?

NEW WORDS OF THE DAY:
encapsulate and *nom de plume*

The ultimate value of life depends upon awareness and the power of contemplation rather than upon mere survival.

—Aristotle, Greek philosopher

List the words that you could use to cultivate your mind, deepen meditation, and achieve a state of heightened awareness. Use those words as departure points to write about your life's journey and what aspects of your life hold the most value for you.

NEW WORD OF THE DAY:
psychodynamics

> *Memory is the diary that we all carry about with us.*
> —OSCAR WILDE, IRISH WRITER AND POET

Create a short rhyme or phrase to aid in recalling a word, expression, or name you were supposed to remember.

NEW WORDS OF THE DAY:
protreptic and *mnemonically*

Any sufficiently advanced technology is indistinguishable from magic.
—ARTHUR C. CLARKE, BRITISH SCIENCE FICTION AUTHOR, INVENTOR, AND FUTURIST

Make a list of the top technological terms or products you would like to know more about. Use each of them in a sentence that describes an action item that you will undertake (such as learning more about that term or product).

1. _____ 6. _____
2. _____ 7. _____
3. _____ 8. _____
4. _____ 9. _____
5. _____ 10. _____

1. _____
2. _____
3. _____
4. _____
5. _____
6. _____
7. _____
8. _____
9. _____
10. _____

NEW WORDS OF THE DAY:
technophobic, *conjurer,* and *cloud computing*

> *We are born at a given moment, in a given place, and, like vintage years of wine, we have the qualities of the year and of the season of which we are born. Astrology does not lay claim to anything more.*
>
> —CARL GUSTAV JUNG,
> SWISS PSYCHIATRIST AND FOUNDER OF ANALYTICAL PSYCHOLOGY

Write a horoscope for each of the twelve astrological signs of the zodiac.

NEW WORDS OF THE DAY:
conjoin and *retrograde*

Don't tell me the moon is shining;
show me the glint of light on broken glass.
—ANTON CHEKHOV, RUSSIAN NOVELIST AND SHORT STORY WRITER

Which evocative words would you choose to paint an atmospheric moonlit scene?

NEW WORDS OF THE DAY:
luminescence and *ethereal*

You gain strength, courage, and confidence by every experience in which you really stop to look fear in the face.
—Eleanor Roosevelt, American First Lady

Which words describe how you feel about the fears you face? Describe those fears.

NEW WORDS OF THE DAY:
bête noir and *abhorrence*

> *We have to sunset programs that no longer work.*
> *We have to eliminate waste and fraud.*
> —Meg Whitman, American Businesswoman

Which workplace words do you find most appealing or appalling? Why?

NEW WORDS OF THE DAY:
arduous and *meticulous*

Destiny is not a matter of chance. It is a matter of choice. It's not a thing to be waited for—it's a thing to be achieved.
—WILLIAM JENNINGS BRYAN, AMERICAN POLITICIAN

Give five reasons why you believe you can (or cannot) control fate and manifest your destiny through intellectual choice.

1.

2.

3.

4.

5.

NEW WORDS OF THE DAY:
predestination and *esoteric*

New ideas are not only the enemies of old ones; they also appear often in an extremely unacceptable form.

—CARL GUSTAV JUNG, SWISS PSYCHIATRIST AND FOUNDER OF ANALYTICAL PSYCHOLOGY

Which new political, religious, philosophical, or theoretical ideologies or concepts have you've explored and either accepted or rejected? Explain.

NEW WORDS OF THE DAY:
demagogue and *futurist*

> *The folly of mistaking a paradox for a discovery, a metaphor for a proof, a torrent of verbiage for a spring of capital truths, and oneself for an oracle is born in us.*
> —Paul Valery, French poet, essayist, and philosopher

Which words would you use to simplify and shorten the above quoted material?

NEW WORDS OF THE DAY:
synoptic and *illogicality*

In the long run, men hit only what they aim at.
—HENRY DAVID THOREAU, AMERICAN AUTHOR, POET, AND NATURALIST

List a total of five new words you will use in conversation during the coming week; using one new word with each of the following:

Your significant other	
Your coworker	
Your best friend	
Your mother	
The grocery store check-out clerk	

NEW WORDS OF THE DAY:
felicitous and *etymology*

*The first forty years of life give us the text;
the next thirty supply the commentary on it.*

—ARTHUR SCHOPENHAUER, GERMAN PHILOSOPHER

What commentary would you write in defense of your life choices, given the years of text you've created thus far?

NEW WORDS OF THE DAY:
querulous, garrulous, and *obstreperous*

Consciousness is either inexplicable illusion, or revelation.
—C. S. LEWIS, IRISH-BORN BRITISH NOVELIST AND ACADEMIC

List five words for elements of ecclesiastical architecture that you might find in the great cathedrals of Europe, for example, and write several paragraphs describing those elements in detail.

NEW WORDS OF THE DAY:
providential and *chimera*

> *Moral excellence comes about as a result of habit. We become just by doing just acts, temperate by doing temperate acts, brave by doing brave acts.*
> —ARISTOTLE, GREEK PHILOSOPHER

List three slang words or epithets you habitually use that you would like to replace and explain why you don't want to be associated with those words.

1. _____
2. _____
3. _____

NEW WORD OF THE DAY:
moral turpitude

> *Life, misfortunes, isolation, abandonment, poverty are battlefields which have their heroes; obscure heroes, sometimes greater than illustrious heroes.*
> —Victor Hugo, French Romantic poet, novelist, and dramatist

List the scourges in the world that are most reprehensible to you and detail your ideas for winning the battle against them.

NEW WORDS OF THE DAY:
de refugiados, *blight,* and *epidemiological*

> *The dogmas of the quiet past are inadequate to the stormy present.*
> —ABRAHAM LINCOLN, AMERICAN PRESIDENT

List the words that best describe the emotions you feel when you are obliged to listen to dogma in conflict with your core beliefs.

NEW WORDS OF THE DAY:
propagandize and *indoctrinate*

*The Third world is not a reality
but an ideology.*

—HANNAH ARENDT, GERMAN-BORN AMERICAN PHILOSOPHER
AND POLITICAL SCIENTIST

What words would you use to differentiate between the third world and the first world? Explain why you chose these words and the meanings behind them.

NEW WORDS OF THE DAY:
dearth, paucity, and *cornucopia*

> *Language is a living, kicking, growing, flitting, evolving reality....*
> —JOHN A. RASSIAS, DARTMOUTH COLLEGE PROFESSOR AND LANGUAGE INSTRUCTION INNOVATOR

What is your favorite old word that has become new, a new word that has been coined to sound like an old word, or a fusion of words into a new word (for example: friend and enemy into frenemy)? Write a short essay on the importance of dynamic language and use your favorite word in the essay.

NEW WORDS OF THE DAY:
RAM, reggaeton, and *soul patch*

*It is not every question that
deserves an answer.*

—PUBLILIUS SYRUS, LATIN WRITER

Name three types of questions that you respond to by circumnavigating, sidestepping, or simply remaining silent and why?

1.

2.

3.

NEW WORDS OF THE DAY:
asinine and *probative*

I think we have to destroy the stereotypes and replace them with archetypes.

—SIR BEN KINGSLEY, BRITISH ACTOR

List two stereotypes you would eliminate and the archetypes you would replace them with.

NEW WORD OF THE DAY:
collective unconscious